Balance
Your
Sh*t

The Chakras

Rachelle Pean, LCSW

CONTENTS

ACKNOWLEDGMENTS

Thank you to Jissel Ravelo for my introduction to the
Chakra System, for our coffee shop conversation where
you told me that God made all of these healing modalities
but she made Henny and twerking too (we can do both),
and for helping me clear my sh*t out. Thank you to my
dear beautiful friends, Karyn, Mekia, and J'vanay for their
LOUD encouragement, loud enough that I put words on
paper instead of keeping them in my head. And an eternal
thank you to my clients and yogi students who are always
teaching me about healing and the resiliency of the human
spirit.

1 HOW TO USE THIS BOOK

So, here's the good news: even if you don't eat granola or kale, even if you don't put crystals in your bra, even if you HATE yoga, there's something in here for you. The guidance from this book will bring you to a healthier you even if you don't believe in this stuff, simply because you are slowing down and paying attention to the different areas of your life. This life places many demands on us and things can move pretty quickly. Bills, family responsibilities, work, planning for the future, thinking about the past....but what about checking in with how we are doing RIGHT NOW? Sometimes, we move along and aren't fully aware of how we're taking care of ourselves, and not acknowledging our own needs can build up and later lead to emotional and physical imbalances.

This book is all about how to care for ourselves by using the lens of the chakras: a 7 point energy system within our energetic aura. *Chakra* is Sanskrit (the ancient

1

language of India) for the word wheel. Picture 7 adorable wheels of energy spinning throughout the center column of your energy body.

What's an energy body? The entire universe is made up of energy, vibrating at different frequencies. This includes our physical cells; picture them all right now, buzzing, exuding out vibrational energy. If you pay close enough attention, you can even feel the vibrations of your physical cells; by getting very still and bringing your attention to your hands, you may be able to feel a heat, a tingling, a pulsation. This is happening throughout your whole body all the time. All these cells together exude energy outwards creates your unique individual aura!

Now imagine the chakras as 7 centers in the middle of your auric field, working hard for you as little filters that help you take in energetic information from the outer world, and help you exude out energy. Everything we come into contact with in our environment has energy as well and exchanges energy with us. Unfortunately, sometimes shit hits the fan, and one or more of our "filters" (chakras) gets clogged. Traumatic experiences, life stress, interactions with different environments and people, all of these things and more can impact our chakras.

That's where this book comes in. Maybe you hear something familiar in some of the "overactive" or "underactive" descriptors, which may mean you have an imbalance in this area. It's important to note that all of us have imbalances sometimes, and the area we need balancing in can change from situation to situation or moment to moment. Please know that if there is an imbalance, you are not broken. You are a beautifully flawed human. A human working towards healing yourself. This guide is a succinct how-to in treating yourself with care, so that you can be great! I mean, you're already the shit, I'm sure of it. But this is how to enhance and flourish.

There's no one way to use this book. You can use this guide to balance all of your chakras sequentially, going through each section one by one. Or you may find that you are feeling imbalanced in one area of your life, and may need to repeat the yoga poses, affirmations, and meditations of a specific chakra daily until you feel steadier in this area of life. You can begin a daily chakra journaling practice, checking in with each energy center and following the prompt questions to write down your reflections. Or maybe, you want your friends to know that you're all spiritual and shit and you can casually throw the word chakra into conversations at brunch.

Enjoy, and may your chakras be aligned. May your physical body be hydrated. May you find silence in the pause between your thoughts. May you move through life like you are made of coconut oil and stardust (because actually you are).

2 THE ROOT CHAKRA

*Our connection to earth, our tribe, and safety in
the world.*

Underactive root chakra: "I can't control this"; feeling helpless, finding it difficult to organize or simplify things in our life, a feeling of not belonging anywhere, frequent fear/distrust/paranoia, having a "lack" mentality (not enough resources).

Overactive root chakra: physical aggression, impulsiveness, irritability, feeling stuck.

Balanced root chakra: Feeling safe, grounded, having an abundance mentality.

Get your roots right! The root chakra is located right at the bottom of the tailbone and coincides with the color red (the color and this chakra vibrate at the same frequency). Our root chakra is what connects us to our "roots", our lower extremities, our connection to the earth. It has to do with our primitive needs: our need to feel connected to our tribe (family stuff), our ability to nourish ourselves (our relationship to food and our physical body) and our beliefs about how safe or dangerous this world is. If any of the "overactive" or "underactive" descriptors rang too close to home, you may need some grounding. Here are some practices that can help:

Yoga Poses:

Mountain Pose:

Stand with your feet hips width distance apart, and root down through the 4 corners of your feet. Imagine that the arch of your foot is like the middle of a suction cup, so that you are firmly grounded on the perimeters of the feet but lifted in the center to draw energy up through the front body. Lift through the heart, lengthen through the crown of the head, and ground down through the back body; the tailbone heavies towards the earth and the heels are strongly connected to the ground. Visualize a red circle spinning right at the base of the tailbone, and roots growing down to the earth.

Chair Pose:

Sit back in an awkward invisible chair. Make sure you can see your toes past your knees! Try to keep length in the spine by keeping the heart open (try not to round the spine), and lift up through the fingertips. Your thighs may be talking to you, but breathe through the burn as you awaken your root chakra.

Squat pose:

Feet are about the width of your yoga mat, toes pointing out. If the heels can't touch the mat that's okay! Pop down into a squat, let your hands come to your heart, with your elbows inside of knees. Heavy the tailbone towards the earth and lift the top of the head to the sky keeping the spine long.

Affirmations:

"I am safe in my body, and my body is my home"

"I have all that I need. I live in abundance and receive support whenever I need it"

"I am **unfuckwith-able**! I am connected to the source, and feel rooted in my strength"

Essential oils:

Sandalwood, cedar, ginger, black pepper, rosewood, cloves, and rosemary

Meditation:

The vibrational sound that correlates with the vibration of the root chakra is the mantra "Lam". Repeat this either in your mind or out loud with every full round of breath while visualizing a spinning red wheel at the base of your tailbone. Know that with every breath you are clearing out this energy center and helping it spin at a balanced rate.

You may also get bare feet onto soil to feel the support of the earth underneath you. If you don't have access to this and are indoors, visualize the floor supporting you, then the foundation of the building, all the way down to the core of the earth. Bring added attention to the points of your body that are connected to the ground and focus on your body being fully supported by this lovely earth.

Self Care for the Root Chakra:

Find a new recipe and cook yourself a delicious
nourishing meal.

Comfort the physical body with soothing tea, curling up
with a blanket, and getting good rest.

Appreciate all your body's abilities. Allow yourself to
express this without it being tainted by society's
unrealistic body image expectations, but rather for what
your body allows you to do in this world. Appreciate all
the senses that are active, your limbs for their abilities,
and your organs for keeping this whole show going!

Exercise! Any kind that gets you fully into your body
and out of your head. Yoga, pilates, walking, dancing,
weight lifting, etc. There is no right exercise, just the one
that fits you.

Journaling Prompts for the Root Chakra:

Where have I learned my messages about whether or not the world is a dangerous place?

What makes me feel safe?

What keeps me grounded?

Am I nurturing my physical needs? If not fully, where can I improve my physical nourishment?

How can I prioritize my personal stability for myself, so that I can be a pillar of strength for others?

Rachelle Pean

----

3 THE SACRAL CHAKRA

Our connection to the flow of life: relationships, sensuality, pleasure, joy, ease, and play

Underactive Sacral Chakra: overly serious, rigid and very routine, difficulty being spontaneous, not feeling creative, intellectualizing (having a hard time being in your body, and all up in your thoughts), shame around sexuality, overly controlling.

Overactive Sacral Chakra: Dependency on a relationship, substance, or pleasurable experience, being ruled by your emotions.

Balanced Sacral Chakra: Feeling a natural flow with our relation to others, nurturing relationships to others, feeling a sense of harmony, comfortable with our sexuality and movements of our bodies.

The Sacral Chakra is all about the water element of our life. It is the ability to get in touch with the flow: the joys and pleasures of this world. It is located by the sacrum, below the navel, in the pelvic area, and is an orange color. It is sometimes called the "Sex Chakra", but has to do with so much more! It's our center of creativity, the divine feminine, and our ability to enjoy play and enjoy relationships to others. If you're feeling overly rigid or maybe flowing TOO much and seeking pleasure excessively, here are some practices that can bring you balance:

Yoga Poses:

Table top hip circles:

Begin in a table top position (hands stacked under the shoulders, knees under the hips). Start to flex the spine in cat and cow pose (belly towards the floor with hips up while looking up, then rounding your upper spine tucking your tailbone and gazing towards the belly button). Begin to move the hips in figure 8's, and let the breath take you away. Let this movement feel good and find freedom in the movement of your hips.

Low lunge:

Come into a low lunge and reach the finger tips up towards the sky. As you feel a stretch in your hip flexors, visualize an orange ball of light spinning in the pelvic area.

Warrior II pose:

While opening the hips, as you inhale that you're drawing energy towards the orange spinning wheel in the pelvis. As you exhale this orange light is spreading outwards through the rest of the body.

Affirmations:

"Creativity radiates to me and through me; I am a creator"

"I release control to get in touch with the flow of life. I can trust that life is unfolding just as it's supposed to!"

"I am in touch with my emotions and see them as valuable messengers. I notice what brings me joy in my life"

"I am a sensual being and enjoy the pleasures of this life"

Essential oils:

Ylang ylang, sandalwood, clary sage, rose, jasmine

Meditation:

The vibrational sound that correlates with the vibration of the sacral chakra is the mantra "Vam". Repeat this either in your mind or out loud with every full round of breath while visualizing a spinning orange wheel in your pelvis.

Imagine this orange energy spreading out throughout your entire body like the flow of water. With every exhale, see this orange field of light getting bigger and bigger, and feel your body slipping into the natural flow and rhythm of your breath. When you are ready to end the meditation, visualize the orange wheel returning back to its normal size, and acknowledge that it is now spinning at a balanced pace.

Self care for the Sacral chakra:

Dance like no one's watching. Bonus points if it's when you're naked. If you're naked you probably should do this if truly there is no one watching. Or not. Live your best life.

Play. Go to an arcade, a playground, or a mystery room with friends. Let go a little!

Create. Write poetry, paint, draw, play music! Even if you don't consider yourself to be a creative, you definitely are a creative being so take time to express that part of yourself.

Journaling prompts for the Sacral Chakra:

What brings me joy in my life? When is the last time I did these things? How can I incorporate more joy into my day to day activities?

Was I encouraged to play when I was younger? Did I feel that I had to be overly responsible? In what areas of my life can I let go and flow?

What are my thoughts around my sexuality? What would it look like if I accepted that I am a sexual being and felt free to express my sexual nature?

Do I see my emotions as scary, or as valuable information? How can I develop a healthier relationship with my emotions?

What are my thoughts around planning vs. spontaneity? Where did I get these lessons from? Are there shifts I can make in these thoughts to create more balance in my life?

_____
_____
_____
_____
_____
_____
_____
_____
_____
_____
_____
_____
_____
_____
_____
_____
_____
_____
_____
_____
_____
_____
_____
_____
_____
_____

4 SOLAR PLEXUS CHAKRA

Your relationship to yourself: your personal power, ego identity, and sense of purpose.

Underactive Solar Plexus Chakra: lack of energy, low self-esteem and confidence, procrastination, indecisiveness, putting others before yourself.

Overactive Solar Plexus Chakra: Type A personality, excessive control over other people or your environment, overly detail oriented, judgmental, jealousy.

Balanced Solar Plexus Chakra: Assert yourself, celebrate yourself, ability to turn your will into external results relatively easily.

Rachelle Pean

The Solar Plexus Chakra is the fire element of life. It's about our fire and passion to be here and leave our own unique fingerprint on this universe showing that we were here. It is located above the navel, towards the center of the torso and is a yellow color. It's your dedication, your willpower, your beliefs about yourself and your ability to get sh*t done. I imagine Oprah, Beyonce, and Gary Vee's Solar Plexus Chakras are all bright and shiny.

If you overly assert your presence in this world and have a hard time slowing down, or if you feel that you shrink into yourself and would like to be more in touch with your personal power, here are some practices that can help:

Yoga Poses:

Power Pose:

Stand with your feet slightly wider than hips width distance. Place your hands on your hips. Close your eyes and breathe; feel the power and aliveness in your body. Imagine a yellow spinning wheel located right at the center of your torso as you do this.

Boat Pose:

Come to balancing on your sit bones and lift the shins parallel to the floor. Allow your chest to remain open and reach the arms forward. Feel how strong you are, and bring your attention to the Solar Plexus chakra as you visualize it spinning.

Bow Pose:

Laying on the belly, bend the knees and reach back to the ankles. Kick into the hands as you open through the chest; remaining strong in the core but opening through the chest and the shoulders.

Affirmations:

"I stand in my personal power. I am worthy of acceptance just as I am; I am the shit!"

"I seek opportunities for my personal growth, because I deserve it."

"I stand up for myself and my personal needs"

"I am a unique powerful being who is worthy and deserving of making my mark in this world"

Essential oils:
Black pepper, cedarwood, cinnamon, clove, coriander, cypress, geranium, ginger.

Meditation:

The vibrational sound that correlates with the vibration of the solar plexus chakra is the mantra "Ram". Repeat this either in your mind or out loud with every full round of breath while visualizing a spinning yellow wheel in the abdomen. Place both hands here as this yellow ball spins and powerful energy grows, spreading empowerment throughout your entire body. You may want to imagine yourself making that assertive decision you've been wanting to make, or visualize you entering a specific situation you'd like to overcome with this newfound personal power. Get very specific when visualizing this and see it through from the beginning all the way to the end.

Self care for the Solar Plexus:

Begin that project you've been putting off. Start just
with one step.

Celebrate your accomplishments thus far: write them
down. Give yourself credit and really acknowledge
your hard work.

Seek out knowledge: read a book simply for the sake
of learning and growing, find a new hobby to delve
into, a skill you want to sharpen, maybe even pursue
learning a new language. If YouTube taught me how
to tie a Windsor knot, you can definitely enhance
your learning self for the free!

Journal prompts for the Solar Plexus Chakra:

What has my relationship to authority been? How comfortable am I with authority and asserting myself?

What is my relationship with having to control the process and/or my environment?

What are my beliefs around personal power? (Particularly for women; have you learned that to assert your power is not feminine? etc.)

What negative messages did I receive about myself? What are new positive beliefs I can begin to tell myself to build my inner power?

Do I avoid challenges? If so, why? How can I begin to take more risks and approach challenging situations?

How do I feel about myself? Do I like myself? How can I show myself the same love and appreciation that I show those I care about?

Rachelle Pean

----

5 THE HEART CHAKRA

Bridges earthly desires and spiritual expansion.
The center for love and compassion.

Underactive Heart Chakra: Holding grudges, withdrawn from others, jealousy, fear of intimacy.

Overactive Heart Chakra: Difficulty with boundaries, lack of discernment in relationships, codependency.

Balanced Heart Chakra: Open to receive and give love, appreciating the beauty in life, seeing beyond the ego and having compassion for others.

The Heart Chakra is midpoint in the chakras located right at the center of the chest and is a green color. With 3 energy centers below and 3 above, it is the connection between our worldly self and our spiritual self. It is the center of love for the self and others. Did you know that when there is a significant heartbreak, literally the fibers of our physical heart can be impacted? It is the same with our energetic heart center. Our Heart Chakra deals with our ability to receive and give unconditional love, our beliefs around boundaries between ourselves and others, and can be significantly impacted by heartbreak, betrayal, or loss.

Yoga Poses:

Cobra Pose:

Laying on your stomach, press through the tops of the feet to activate your quads and shins. Engage your core to protect your lower back, and with hands outside of ribs lengthen through the crown of the head as you pick up your head and heart and lift the head and heart forward and up.

Puppy Pose:

Come to kneeling with the hips stacked over the knees. Walk the arms forward and let the forehead sink towards your mat or a yoga block. Keep the hips stacked over the knees as you let your heart soften towards the mat, relaxing the weight of your upper body towards the earth without forcing your weight down. Breathe here as your chest opens up and the shoulders begin to relax.

Bow Pose:

Laying on the belly, bend the knees and reach back to the ankles. Kick into the hands as you open through the chest; remaining strong in the core but opening through the chest and the shoulders.

Affirmations:

(Look yourself in the mirror for this one, I mean dead in the eyes, and say it as many times as you need to!): "I love you. I'm sorry. Please forgive me. Thank you." (this is the Hawaiian Ho'oponopono Forgiveness Mantra).

"I am grace and love, and see grace in love in the world around me."

"My heart is filled with joy and compassion. I am grateful for each and every moment I'm here on this earth."

"I choose love. I choose forgiveness. I am whole, and I LOVE all of me."

Essential oils:

Bergamot, cypress, geranium, jasmine, lavender, lemon

Rachelle Pean

Meditation:
The vibrational sound that correlates with the
vibration of the heart chakra is the mantra "Yam".
Repeat this either in your mind or out loud with every
full round of breath while visualizing a spinning green
wheel in the heart.
Place your left hand on your heart, and your right
hand on top of the left. With every in breath, feel
yourself drawing in loving energy right to your heart
center. With every out breath, feel this green energy of
love spreading throughout your entire being. Send this
love beyond your physical body, and let it fill the
room. As you inhale and exhale, visualize sending this
loving energy out to fill the entire world.

Self care for the Heart Chakra:

Pamper yourself! Create a love playlist just for yourself. Run yourself a bath, add in soothing scents, and give yourself a full body massage with oils. Love up on YOU.

Write yourself an in depth love letter. Write it to the parts of yourself you dislike sometimes. That inner critic? Write to him/her about how you understand why they exist. Practice unconditional acceptance of ALL of you.

Help someone who is having a hard time (by listening, by donating your time, however you can). Feel what it feels like to give just for the sake of giving.

Set boundaries: say NO to others more often to say yes to yourself. Yup, that's it, that's taking care of yourself!

Journaling prompts for the Heart Chakra:

What were the messages you received about love during your childhood?

What is your "love language"? How do you know when others care about you? How do you express your care and love to others?

Do you place conditions on your self love? (Example: you only approve of yourself when you have accomplished something, but not when you are cranky, tired, just failed at something, etc.). Imagine that you are good enough, NO MATTER WHAT. What does that feel like?

What are 10 things that you absolutely love about yourself right now?

What kind of evening would you plan to celebrate someone you love dearly? When is the last time you did those things for yourself?

Who are you SO grateful for? Think about all the things that had to happen in the universe for that person to enter your path.

_____
_____
_____
_____
_____
_____
_____
_____
_____
_____
_____
_____
_____
_____
_____
_____
_____
_____
_____
_____
_____
_____
_____
_____
_____
_____
_____
_____
_____
_____
_____

6 THROAT CHAKRA

Speaking your truth, projecting your creativity and purpose out into the world.

Underactive Throat Chakra: difficulty following through on your word, telling lies frequently, secretive, difficulty speaking up for yourself, poor communication.

Overactive Throat Chakra: gossiping, nonstop talking, verbally aggressive, difficulty keeping secrets.

Balanced Throat Chakra: authenticity, expressing the highest truth of who you are, good sense of timing and communication with others.

Rachelle Pean

The Throat Chakra is located at the throat and is a blue color. It is our center of authentic expression of who we truly are. It has to do with our ability to communicate in a timely and effective manner. Sometimes, we have experiences that teach us our voices don't matter. Or we feel we may have to be louder in order to be acknowledged. These experiences and others can create imbalances in the throat chakra. Here are some practices to balance your sh*t out!

Yoga Poses:

Fish pose:

Lay on your back, puff up your chest and prop your upper back up using your forearms, and bring the crown of your head to the mat.

Camel pose:

Come to kneeling with knees hips width distance apart. Stack your hips over your knees and heart over your hips. Bring your hands to your lower back and reach your elbows towards each other. Begin to look towards the back wall and let your head cradle in your shoulder blades.

Neck stretches:

Let the head roll in circles slowly, stretching all sides of the neck. Take your time as you do this and listen to your breathing. Make sure to roll your head in the opposite direction as well.

Affirmations:

"FUCK". (No for real, try it. Use bass in your voice and puff out your chest).

"I am comfortable with silence, and speak when I have an authentic truth to tell"

"My voice matters; no one can express my truth but me"

"I claim and honor that I am here to deliver a message that others want to hear"

Essential oils:

Frankincense, ylang ylang, sandalwood, rose, jasmine, neroli

Meditation:

The vibrational sound that correlates with the vibration of the throat chakra is the mantra "Ham". Repeat this either in your mind or out loud with every full round of breath while visualizing a spinning blue wheel in the throat. As this light spins brighter and brighter, acknowledge that you are releasing barriers between you and speaking your highest truth. Upon completion of the meditation, know that you have cleansed your throat chakra and it is spinning at a perfectly balanced rate.

Rachelle Pean

Self care for the throat chakra:

Write your truth: be brutally honest about your thoughts
and feelings, uncensored, and just free write for 10
minutes. You'd be surprised at what may come up when
you let your inner voice express itself.

Sing in the shower. Pick one of those songs that makes
you feel like you can SANG. Do it. At the top of your
lungs, with your shampoo bottle as your mic.

Practice being vulnerable about how you really feel with
people you trust. If you're one to hold it all in, don't for
once. See what happens when you let people in on your
struggles, and speak your truth.
Speak up for yourself. Even if it doesn't keep the peace.
Even if others won't like it. Practice acting like your
voice matters, because it does!

Journaling prompts:

How comfortable am I with communicating my truth?
What are my barriers to communicating what's important
to me?

What lessons did my childhood teach me about how
valuable my voice is? In my family, did I feel my voice was
heard? How did I communicate my needs/feelings when I
was younger? How did others' communicate?

What lessons about communication from my childhood do
I want to keep? What do I want to let go of?

What spaces can I create for myself to express my
authentic self (i.e. expressing yourself more to trusted
people, writing down your truth, etc.)? Are there any
changes I want to make in my communication patterns?

Rachelle Pean

----

7 THIRD EYE CHAKRA

Knowledge of self, intuition, connection to wisdom and insight

Underactive Third Eye Chakra: feeling stuck in the day to day without an overarching sense of direction and purpose, lack of clarity, rejection of "bigger picture" ideas such as spirituality.

Overactive Third Eye Chakra: having delusions, difficulty telling reality from psychic fantasies.

Balanced Third Eye Chakra: you are in touch with your intuition, wisdom of knowing the bigger picture, able to see beyond distractions in life.

The Third Eye Chakra is located in between the brows and is an indigo color. It is our center of intuition; of sight within and without. From here we understand our place in this bigger world, our purpose, but also we understand our true inner voice. Sometimes we feel like we can't trust our intuition, we seek validation from others before trusting ourselves, or we just feel stuck in life. These are all signs to work towards balancing the Third Eye Chakra!

Yoga Poses:

Child's pose:

One of my favs. Your knees are about as wide as the mat, and you lay your arms and head down to the mat as your hips settle back by your heels. Listen to the sound of your breath, and notice where your inhales travel to so you can really drop into your body for this pose.

Mountain Pose:

Standing mountain pose with thumbs to your third eye chakra

Shoulder stand:

Laying on your back, rock and roll your hips into your hands and then stack the feet over the hips with legs fully extended towards the ceiling. Close your eyes and look within to your third eye center; notice any swirling colors, dots, or images. (If this is your first time trying this pose, please do so with the guidance of a yoga teacher).

Affirmations:

"I have a vision for my life and am manifesting my reality step by step"

"I trust myself. When I slow down, I realize only I have the answers I am looking for"

"My possibilities are unlimited"

"I am knowing. I am pure presence. I am in the here and now"

Essential oils:

Angelica root, bay laurel, clary sage, cypress, elemin, frankincense, juniper.

Rachelle Pean

Meditation:

The vibrational sound that correlates with the
vibration of the third eye chakra is the mantra "Aum".
Repeat this either in your mind or out loud with every
full round of breath while visualizing a spinning indigo
wheel in between the brows. As this light spins brighter
and brighter, acknowledge that you are accessing your
connection to your inner world. Turn a razor sharp
focus on your inner world, sensing how your
consciousness feels inside of your body. Let this space
expand outward. Sit within this place of knowing, of
seeing, both yourself and the bigger picture. Trust that
you are fine tuning yourself as the intuitive being that
you were born to be.

Self care for the third eye:

Begin a dream journal and fill it out in as many details as you remember first thing in the morning! Our dreams are ways that our intuition speaks to us, take some time to reflect on what they're saying.

Get you some tarot cards; even if you don't fully believe in this stuff. Try asking the cards a question and getting in touch with your inner voice's reactions to what cards come up.

Practice saying no without an explanation. Trust your gut!

Before making any big decisions, bring up the situation in your mind's eye. Practice sitting with yourself and sense how your body feels if you were to say "yes" or "no". Visualize different outcomes and really FEEL what that feels like in your body. Trust that feeling.

Journaling prompts:

What helps me feel most connected to my intuition?

Do I often second guess myself? If so, why do I think that
is? Was I encouraged to trust my intuition growing up? Did
I learn that the answers are outside of myself or that I have
the answers?

What are my experiences with being in touch with other
spiritual realms?

Have I had vivid dreams or felt a gut instinct "knowing"
about certain things? If fear/anxiety surrounds these
experiences, how can I release fear of this knowing and
embrace it as a part of my being?

_____
_____
_____
_____
_____
_____
_____
_____
_____
_____
_____

Balance Your Sh*t

Rachelle Pean

8 THE CROWN CHAKRA

Higher consciousness, universal energy,
spirituality, divine power

Underactive Crown Chakra: depression,
apathy, disconnection with purpose

Overactive Crown Chakra: disconnection
with the body, obsessive attachment to
spiritual matters

Balanced Crown Chakra: Being fully present
and connected to the highest self, feeling
awareness of collective consciousness,
freedom from limiting patterns and habits

Rachelle Pean

The Crown Chakra is located at the crown of the
head and is bright white light. This center is our
connection to universal energy and higher
consciousness. This is the place of our connection to
the entire UNIVERSE. Blockages can result with
feeling disconnected from the bigger picture of us all
having meaning on this earth in this lifetime. If this
area is too activated, we cannot feel "of our body",
forget to nourish our bodies appropriately, or have
difficulty feeling grounded. The Crown Chakra serves
as the portal for energy to come through and radiate
through the rest of our chakras!

Yoga Poses:

Headstand:

ONLY if this is already in your practice. If you are new to yoga go
with the other listed poses for now.

Standing mountain pose "lotus hands" on the crown of the head:

Place hands together with thumbs touching and pinkies touching.
Leave a space between the hands and the place the heels of the hands
with a slight opening on the crown of the head. Close your eyes and
breathe as you visualize warm bright light funneling down through the
crown.

Resting pose:

BEST POSE EVER. Lay there. Yup, that's it. Turn it up a notch by
relaxing the palms and allowing them to be open towards the sky.
Allow your body to be fully supported by the ground beneath you. As
you breathe in and out, feel the golden light of consciousness flowing
down through the crown of the head filling the entire body.

Affirmations:

"I am of the universe and receive divine guidance at all times"

"I belong. I am truth. I am unlimited consciousness"

"The fact that I was born, that I am here today as I am, is a miracle. I am in touch with the flow of the universe and my purpose"

Essential oils:
Lavender, rosewood, vetiver, frankincense

Meditation:

The vibrational sound that correlates with the vibration of the
third eye chakra is the mantra "Om". Repeat this either in
your mind or out loud with every full round of breath while
visualizing golden white light coming down through the
crown of your head. With every inhale, visualize this energy
flowing through your body more and more, and as you
exhale feel each cell this light touches buzz with warm healing
energy. Continue this meditation until you entire body is
filled with this energy, and visualize yourself radiating a
golden healing glow outwards.

Self care for the crown chakra:

Create a gratitude list. Get specific about all the things that had to align for you to experience that person, place, thing, or experience you are grateful for.

Call 2 people you love (nope, not texting, call them!) and tell them 3 reasons why you love them.

Go outside in nature. Leave your phone behind. Find some trees, and begin to observe them. Like really SEE them. Think about how connected you are to nature; breathing in what trees breathe out, and vice versa! They are our external lungs. It's really amazing when you think about it.

Journaling prompts:

You being here is no accident. What is your "why"?
Your motivation for doing what you do every day?

When do you feel most connected to your purpose?

At what times in your life did you feel most
connected to the flow of life and the bigger picture?

Write about your highest self. How does he/she
think, behave, feel? Can you begin to consult your
highest self when you encounter a life challenge?

What does it mean to have an awakening?

Rachelle Pean

_____

_____

_____

_____

_____

_____

_____

_____

_____

_____

_____

_____

_____

_____

_____

_____

_____

_____

_____

_____

_____

_____

_____

_____

_____

9 CONGRATULATIONS, YOU ALIGNED YOUR SH*T!

Tada! **YOU'RE FIXED.** Just kidding, you were never broken you beautiful human. This book doesn't have the answers, and no one else has the answers for what you need but you. I hope this guide served as a reminder (I say reminder because, we **KNOW** and we always knew, but sometimes we forget) of what you need and helped you listen to your inner voice.

I'm grateful that your journey brought you to this book. This balancing work, this self care work, this learning ourselves work, is an ongoing journey. It's not linear either; sometimes we revisit areas. Sometimes we break down again and build ourselves back up. The goal isn't "completion" or having it all together, because that's not real. The goal is to realize that only we are responsible for our healing, and that all we need is within us. As we learn and balance what's within us, we realize that what's within us is also in others. Namaste.

Rachelle Pean

Sources:

http://www.chakras.info/

The Chakra Bible by Patricia Mercer

http://www.chopra.com/

Made in the USA
Columbia, SC
26 July 2021